W9-AMP-837

CORE SKILLS

GRAPH IT
READING CHARTS AND GRAPHS

Gillian Gosman

PowerKiDS
press
New York

Published in 2015 by The Rosen Publishing Group, Inc.
29 East 21st Street, New York, NY 10010

First Edition

Editor: Caitie McAneney
Book Design: Mickey Harmon

Photo Credits: Cover (class) Monkey Business Images/Shutterstock.com; cover (background) Attitude/Shutterstock.com; pp. 3–32 (dot backgrounds) vlastas/Shutterstock.com; p. 4 leung chopan/Shutterstock.com; p. 5 Alexander Raths/Shutterstock.com; p. 6 Andrey_Popov/Shutterstock.com; p. 7 USBFCO/Shutterstock.com; p. 10 kazoka/Shutterstock.com; p. 11 Quang Ho/Shutterstock.com; p. 13 mkos83/Shutterstock.com; p. 15 (butterfly life cycle) snapgalleria/Shutterstock.com; p. 15 (pyramid outline) dalmingo/Shutterstock.com; p. 17 bikeriderlondon/Shutterstock.com; p. 18 mhatzapa/Shutterstock.com; pp. 20–21 Africa Studio/Shutterstock.com; p. 23 (grilled cheese) Antonio Gravante/Shutterstock.com; p. 23 (tacos) Hurst Photo/Shutterstock.com; p. 23 (salad greens) Blan-k/Shutterstock.com; p. 25 AVAVA/Shutterstock.com; p. 26 Artush/Shutterstock.com; pp. 27, 30 Minerva Studio/Shutterstock.com; p. 29 Compassionate Eye Foundation/Robert Daly/OJO Images/Iconica/Getty Images.

Library of Congress Cataloging-in-Publication Data

Gosman, Gillian.
Graph it: reading charts and graphs / by Gillian Gosman.
p. cm. — (Core skills)
Includes index.
ISBN 978-1-4777-7378-9 (pbk.)
ISBN 978-1-4777-7379-6 (6-pack)
ISBN 978-1-4777-7377-2 (library binding)
1.Graphic methods — Juvenile literature. I. Gosman, Gillian. II. Title.
QA90.G67 2015
001.4—d23

Manufactured in the United States of America

CPSIA Compliance Information: Batch #CW15PK: For Further Information contact Rosen Publishing, New York, New York at 1-800-237-9932

CONTENTS

INTRODUCING CHARTS AND GRAPHS

How can you present information in an easy and eye-catching way? You can use illustrations such as charts and graphs. To many readers, charts and graphs are more interesting and easier to read than blocks of text. They grab the reader's attention and make difficult **concepts** addressed in the text easier to understand.

Charts and graphs are all around us, so it's important to learn how to read and understand them. Teachers may ask you to present information in the form of a chart or graph, so it's important to learn how to create them, too.

The terms "chart" and "graph" are sometimes used to describe the same thing. However, in this book, we'll use them to describe two different kinds of **diagrams**. Each term will be defined in a following chapter.

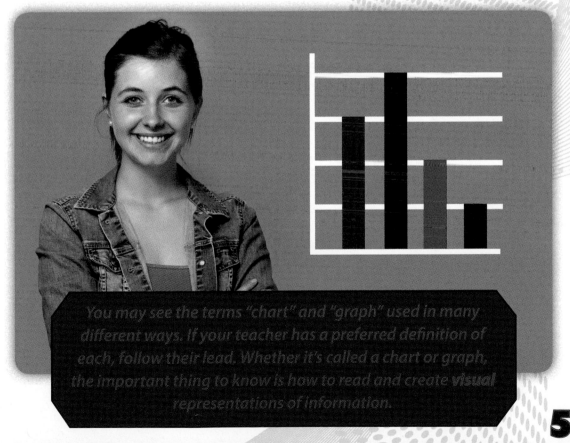

You may see the terms "chart" and "graph" used in many different ways. If your teacher has a preferred definition of each, follow their lead. Whether it's called a chart or graph, the important thing to know is how to read and create **visual** representations of information.

USES FOR CHARTS AND GRAPHS

Charts and graphs are used in many school subjects. Your math teacher may ask you to find information from charts and graphs to solve problems. You'll find them in your science and social studies textbooks, too. You may even use them in language arts to understand the connections between characters or events in a book.

Charts and graphs can be used to illustrate real-world trends. The line graph on page 7 shows numbers increasing, which indicates an upward trend.

Learning how to read charts and graphs will prepare you for reading and creating them in the real world. Your doctor may use a graph to explain health-related data, such as height and weight. News outlets—on television, online, and in print—use charts and graphs to illustrate the data behind an important story. A weatherman might use a graph to show changes in temperature during a week.

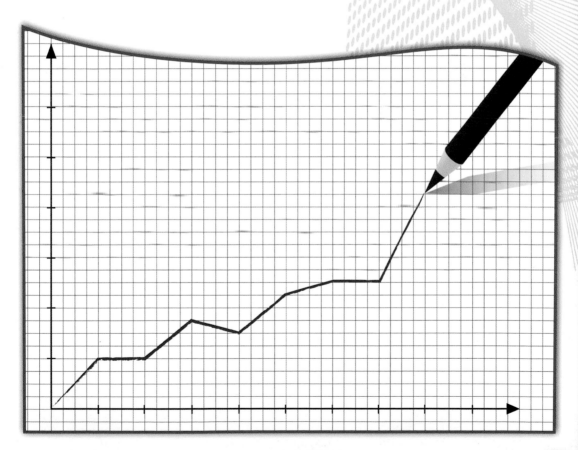

WHEN DO I NEED A CHART?

A chart is a diagram that shows the relationships between various parts or elements. Charts use lines, labels, arrows, and other connectors to **link** these elements. The structure of the chart and the way the elements are represented tell us something important about their relationships to one another.

In social studies, you might create a chart called a timeline to track a series of events through history. In science class, you could use a chart to illustrate the **hierarchy** of groups, such as food groups. You might use a chart to explain how different animal **species** were once related. In each of these cases, the chart helps the reader understand something important about how these events, objects, people, or species are related to one another.

A timeline is a chart that illustrates the **chronological** relationship of events. It can help answer the question "What happened first?" This food chart helps answer the question "Which foods should I eat the most?"

Timeline of the American Revolution

December 1776
George Washington crosses the Delaware River with troops.

May 1780
Charleston, South Carolina, falls to British troops.

April 1775
War breaks out in Battles of Lexington and Concord.

February 1778
France signs a treaty with the United States.

October 1781
British army surrenders at Yorktown.

A Balanced Diet

Fruits

Grains

Vegetables

Protien

Dairy

CHOOSING A CHART

Charts come in many shapes—triangles, rectangles, and even circles! A circle chart is ideal for illustrating a cycle of events, such as a life cycle. For example, a circle chart could follow a frog as it starts as an egg and then turns into a tadpole, young frog, and then adult frog, before laying its own eggs.

A Venn diagram is a chart made up of two or more circles, each representing a different element. Similarities between two or more elements are shown in the areas where the circles overlap. Qualities held by only one element are shown in the areas where the circles don't overlap. For example, you might have a Venn diagram that shows the similarities and differences between two books you read.

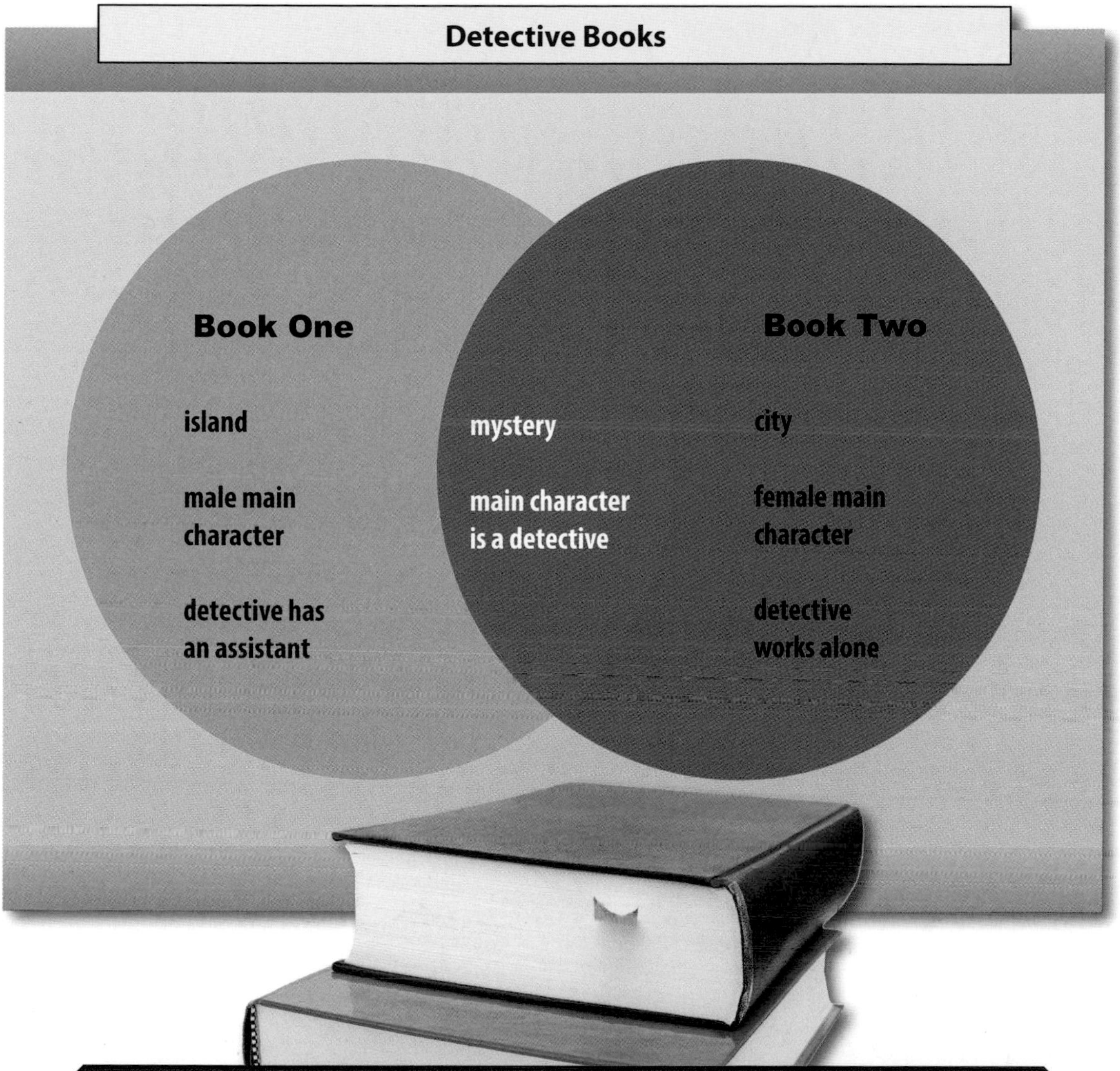

Detective Books

Book One

island

male main
character

detective has
an assistant

mystery

main character
is a detective

Book Two

city

female main
character

detective
works alone

This Venn diagram shows the similarities and differences between two books. Look to the sections that don't overlap to find differences. "Book One" is set on an island, while "Book Two" is set in a city. Look to the overlap section to find similarities. They're both mystery books and have a detective as the main character.

READING CHARTS

Imagine you've come across a strange diagram in your textbook. You think it might be a chart, but how can you tell what it means? Some charts are hard to read because they represent relationships that are difficult to understand.

First, read all labels. What's the title? What are the elements? Consider the placement of each element in relation to the others. Elements that are at the bottom of the chart might be "less than" in some way, while elements at the top of the chart may be of greater value. Likewise, elements at the center of a circle chart may be more important than those on the outer edges. In a timeline, elements to the left or top occur before those to the right or bottom.

QUICK TIP

Once you have determined the relationships between the chart's elements, think about what you see. Do the relationships presented in the chart make sense? What further conclusions can you draw?

12

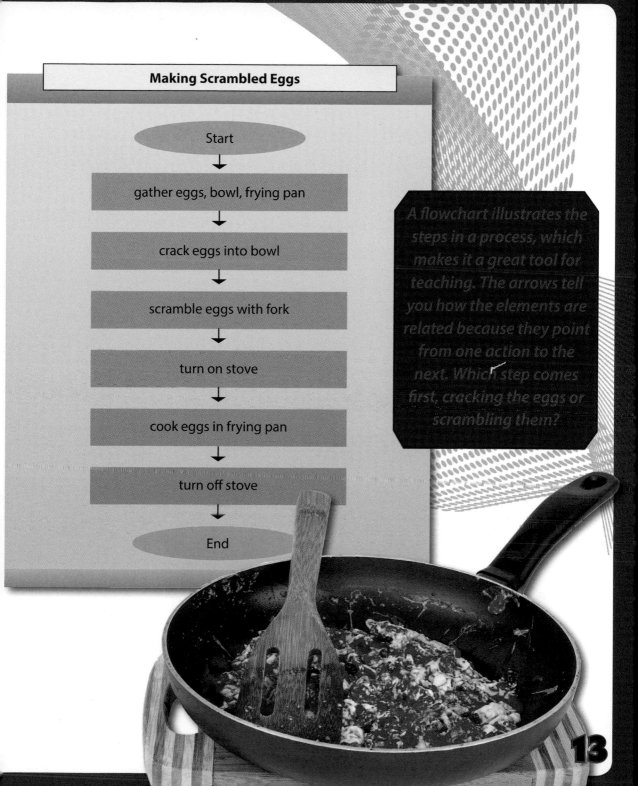

Making Scrambled Eggs

Start

↓

gather eggs, bowl, frying pan

↓

crack eggs into bowl

↓

scramble eggs with fork

↓

turn on stove

↓

cook eggs in frying pan

↓

turn off stove

↓

End

A flowchart illustrates the steps in a process, which makes it a great tool for teaching. The arrows tell you how the elements are related because they point from one action to the next. Which step comes first, cracking the eggs or scrambling them?

CHART IT!

How can you make your own chart? If you have a collection of elements that relate to one another in some way, you may have the makings of a chart.

Begin by identifying the elements you would like to include in your chart. Make a list, a word cloud, or a wall of sticky notes—whatever helps you organize your thoughts. Now begin exploring the connections between the elements. If the relationships between these elements are easy to understand, as in a series of chronological events, this step might be easy. But sometimes elements are linked in multiple, **complex** ways. It may take some time to discover which relationships are important and which you'd like to represent in your chart.

Choosing the right shape for your chart is important. Circles suggest a cycle of events or ideas. Arrows suggest that one element leads to another. Triangles generally suggest a hierarchy, such as this pyramid chart about time. It shows that a second is the shortest unit of time.

Different Types of Charts

cycle chart

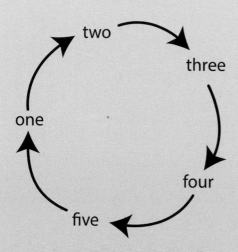

pyramid chart

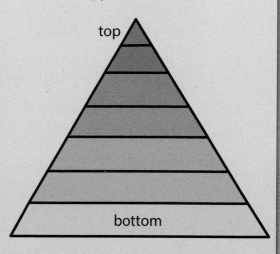

Life Cycle of a Butterfly

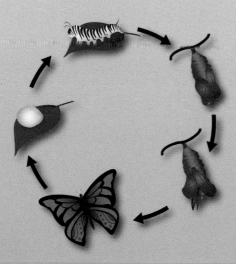

Time

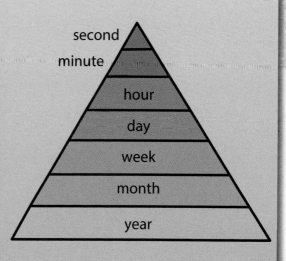

15

TIME FOR GRAPHS

Graphs are diagrams used to illustrate sets of **numerical** data. In most graphs, each measurement—called a data point—is made up of two numbers, and these two numbers are related to each other in some way. For example, if you wanted to show how a person's height is related to their age, you could use a graph. You could also use a graph to show how temperature is related to time of year.

Each of these pairs—height and age, temperature and date—can be illustrated as a single point that represents how the two values relate. The axes of a graph are the lines that cross each other, labeled x and y. The x-axis runs horizontally, or side to side. The y-axis runs vertically, or up and down.

Here's an example of a line graph relating age and height for one person. Age is plotted along the x-axis, and height is plotted along the y-axis. Notice that height depends on age, not the other way around. Look at the graph. How tall was this person at age 9?

GREAT GRAPHS

Common graphs are scatter plots, line graphs, and bar graphs. Line graphs show a collection of related points. Scatter plots show a collection of unrelated points.

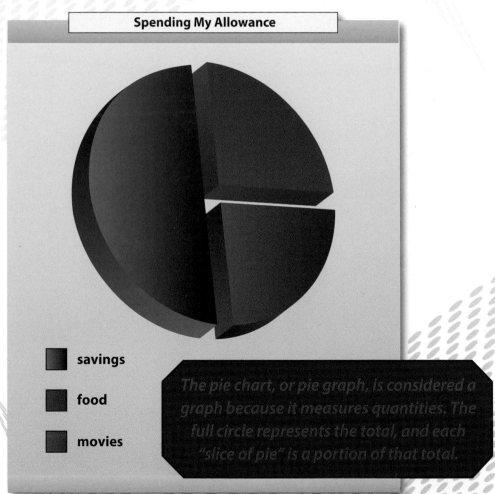

Spending My Allowance

savings

food

movies

The pie chart, or pie graph, is considered a graph because it measures quantities. The full circle represents the total, and each "slice of pie" is a portion of that total.

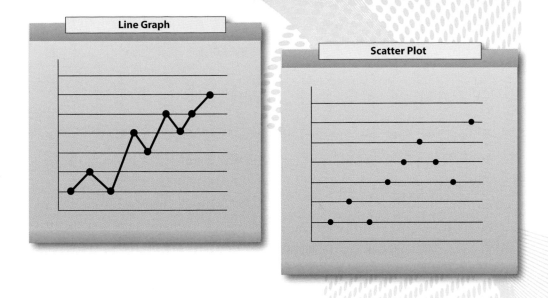

As we've seen on page 17, a line graph can show how one person's height changes with age. A scatter plot can show the **correlation** between measurements of height by age of a large group of people. One person's height is not dependent on any other person's height. However, across the group, a person's height increases with their age. This scatter plot correlation shows that in general, a person's height increases with age.

We might use a bar graph to highlight how many people in a group are certain heights. The x-axis would show height and the y-axis would show the number of people who are that height.

READING GRAPHS

When looking at a graph for the first time, ask yourself the following questions. First, what's represented on the x-axis and y-axis? Look to the labels on the axes to help you find this answer. Second, what are the units of the axes? For example, does the graph measure in years, minutes, inches, or centimeters? Third, what is the **scale** of each axis? For example, does the graph include data points from birth to age seventy or from five years old to seven years old?

Some graphs include a legend, or list of symbols and their meanings. If you see a legend, study it closely.

Just as when reading a chart, perhaps the most important part of reading a graph is drawing conclusions about the information it presents.

QUICK TIP

To draw conclusions about a graph, look for patterns in the graph's structure, values, and data. What can you learn from the graph? What more would you like to know?

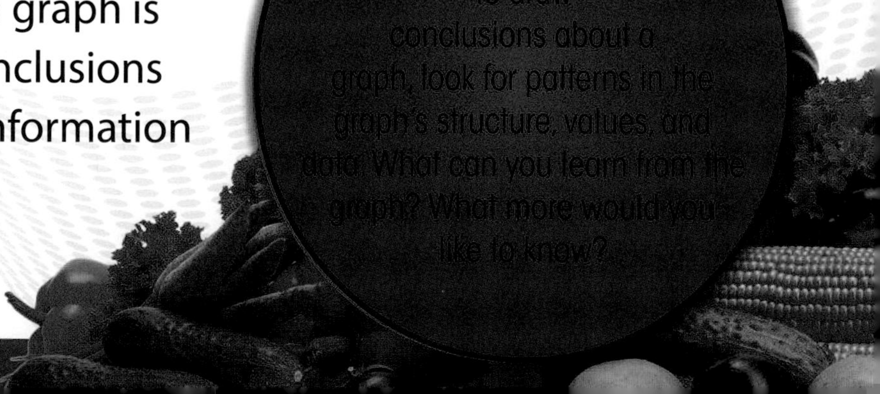

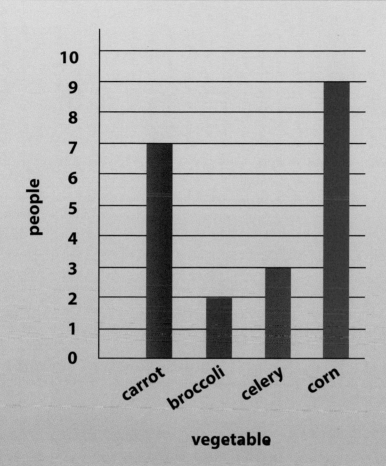

Favorite Vegetables

people

10
9
8
7
6
5
4
3
2
1
0

carrot   broccoli   celery   corn

vegetable

The title of this bar graph tells you it's about favorite vegetables. The x-axis tells you the vegetable, and the y-axis tells you how many people like that vegetable. You can tell that more people like corn than celery. Fewer people like broccoli than carrots. What other conclusions can you draw from the bar graph?

GRAPH IT!

Many computer programs, such as Microsoft Excel, come with graph creation tools. These programs have you enter values for each data point into a table. A table is a rectangle with columns and rows that create cells, or smaller rectangles. Even if you're not using a computer program, it's wise to record and organize your data in a table. Tables come in all sizes and can be simple or complex. Once you make your table, the program can make it into a graph.

If you're drawing your graph by hand, you'll need to decide which variable is independent and, therefore, should be graphed along the x-axis. Also, decide which variable is dependent and should be graphed along the y-axis.

QUICK TIP

Choose the format of the graph carefully. It's usually best to stay simple. Enter the data into the electronic table slowly and pay attention to details. One wrong number can make your graph a confusing jumble.

School Lunch Options	
lunches	people
salad	10
grilled cheese	4
tacos	6

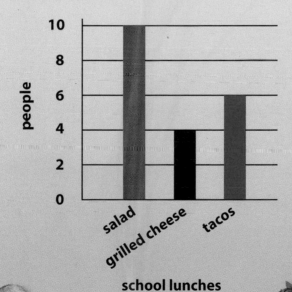

RESEARCH PAPERS

In school, you may be asked to **research** a topic and write about your findings. Good research sources include books, articles, and educational websites. After you gather information, you can present it in written and visual formats. You can make your own chart or graph, or present one that was created by someone else. If you use someone else's graph, be sure to **cite** it.

When making a chart or graph for a research paper, choose the ideas or data sets that are most difficult to understand without diagrams. Any information presented in a chart or graph should also be in the written body of the paper. The chart or graph should be an aid to understanding the text.

You may want to print graphs and charts as a full page in your research paper, so important labels can be easily read. However, your teacher may want something different. Ask your teacher what they prefer.

ORAL PRESENTATIONS

Certain computer programs, such as Microsoft PowerPoint and Prezi, make it easy to make a presentation that stands out. You might use one of these programs to help you with an oral presentation, which is a presentation you make aloud.

If you're describing an upward trend in your presentation, you might want to include a line graph that illustrates that trend.

If it would help your audience in understanding an important idea or data set, consider including a chart or graph in your presentation. Be sure that any labels, symbols, colors, and patterns can be seen from a distance. Explain these visual aids to your audience slowly and clearly. Try to face your audience as much as possible, not your visual aids. When using a graph or chart created by another person, be sure to cite your source directly in your presentation.

SUBJECT AREAS

Chances are, you've encountered charts and graphs in most subject areas, including math, science, social studies, and language arts. When you see these diagrams, ask yourself why the author or teacher has chosen to include them. What information, trends, or relationships are they trying to show?

Then, consider this additional challenge: How can you use charts and graphs as a way to better understand a subject area? For example, how can you illustrate relationships between characters in a book using a chart? How can you suggest a relationship among scientific data using a graph? How can you explain a complex process, such as cooking dinner, using a chart? Practice using visual figures to understand and remember important information.

Some people learn information best through hands-on learning, while others learn best by hearing information read aloud. Some people are visual learners, which means they learn best by looking at a diagram or picture. Charts and graphs are great tools for visual learners!

VISUAL TOOLS

Charts and graphs are useful tools for understanding and presenting information. Computers, smart boards, and film have become popular ways to give presentations. Today, many people would rather see information in a visual way than written out. It has become important to keep presentations visually interesting. This makes it important to practice reading and creating charts and graphs.

Do you learn best reading information as text? Or do you find charts and graphs make information easier to understand? If so, you might be a visual learner. When you grow up, you may want to find a career that uses charts and graphs. Scientists, engineers, and mathematicians use charts and graphs all the time! Can you think of other careers that might use charts and graphs?

GLOSSARY

chronological (krah-nuh-LAH-jih-kuhl) Based on time order.

cite (SYT) To give credit to a source.

complex (kahm-PLEHKS) Hard to understand.

concept (KAHN-sehpt) An idea.

correlation (kohr-uh-LAY-shun) A relationship or connection between two or more things.

diagram (DY-uh-gram) A drawing that shows how elements are arranged or related.

hlerarchy (HY-uh-rahr-kee) A ranking of people, animals, or groups by power or importance.

link (LINK) To connect two things.

numerical (noo-MEHR-ih-kuhl) Have to do with numbers.

research (REE-suhrch) To study a subject deeply.

scale (SKAYL) The range of numbers on an axis.

species (SPEE-sheez) A group of living things that are all the same kind.

visual (VIH-zhuh-wuhl) Having to do with sight or illustration.

INDEX

WEBSITES

Due to the changing nature of Internet links, PowerKids Press has developed an online list of websites related to the subject of this book. This site is updated regularly. Please use this link to access the list: www.powerkidslinks.com/cosk/grap